#595

Maggie & Pierre

MAGGIE & PIERRE

—a fantasy of love, politics and the media

a play by Linda Griffiths with Paul Thompson

Talonbooks • Vancouver • Los Angeles • 1980

copyright © 1980 Linda Griffiths with Paul Thompson

published with assistance from the Canada Council

Talonbooks   *Talonbooks*
201 1019 East Cordova   *P.O. Box 42720*
Vancouver   *Los Angeles*
British Columbia V6A 1M8   *California 90042*
Canada   *U.S.A.*

This book was typeset by Mary Schendlinger at Pulp Press, designed by David Robinson and printed by Friesen for Talonbooks.

The text photographs were taken by Glen E. Erikson.

First printing: October 1980

Canadian Cataloguing in Publication Data

Griffiths, Linda, 1953-
    Maggie & Pierre

    ISBN 0-88922-182-0 (pbk.)

    1. Trudeau, Pierre Elliott, 1919-   - Drama.
2. Trudeau, Margaret, 1948-   - Drama.
I. Thompson, Paul, 1939-   II. Title.
PS8563.R53M3   C812'.54   C81-091027-6
PR9199.3.G74M3

Maggie & Pierre previewed in the Backspace at Theatre Passe Muraille in Toronto, Ontario on November 30, 1979. It opened in the Mainspace at Theatre Passe Muraille on February 14, 1980, with the following cast:

Henry	Linda Griffiths
Maggie	Linda Griffiths
Pierre	Linda Griffiths

Directed by Paul Thompson
Set and Costume Design by Paul Kelman
Lighting Design by Jim Plaxton

More or less, we're all afflicted with the psychology of the voyeur. Not in a strictly clinical or criminal sense, but in our whole physical and emotional stance before the world. Whenever we seek to break this spell of passivity, our actions are cruel and awkward and generally obscene like an invalid who has forgotten how to walk.

Jim Morrison
The Lords and New Creatures Poems

Introduction

After a certain length of time performing in a one-person show, interior dialogue becomes the most natural way of thinking. Hence, the form of my introduction:

Where did you get the idea to write Maggie & Pierre?

The original idea was Paul Thompson's. A group of actors, myself included, were working on a comedy about five English people's experiences in Québec that was performed in French to Québecois audiences in Montréal. It was called "Les Maudits Anglais." In rehearsal, I began fooling around with a Pierre Trudeau character and one day Thompson said, "That's it. That's your one-person show. You play both of them." I thought he was out of his mind. A year later, we began rehearsal.

You worked for many months on the initial research for this play. How did this develop?

My initial research was to talk to people, anyone that had an opinion—and it seemed that everyone had an opinion. I even went down to Eaton's Centre in Toronto with a tape recorder and asked people how they felt about the Trudeaus. Then, I did the traditional things: read books, not just on them or by them, but books on Canadian politics and the media. I spoke to friends of theirs, journalists; anyone who knew them directly and was willing to talk to me. I didn't have any contacts at first, but gradually the feelers went out and I was getting suggestions of people to talk to. I got into the CTV film library and the National Archives in Ottawa and watched film clips of interviews, campaign speeches, sometimes running them five or six times. I talked my way into the CBC library and read a foot and a half of newspaper clippings. I made three trips to Ottawa to get the feel of the place. I did things like standing outside of 24 Sussex Drive for about an hour, trying to imagine what it would be like to live there. On my third trip to Ottawa, Parliament had just opened and I talked my way into the cocktail party circuit and went to the Governor-General's Ball. It was there I was able to meet Pierre Trudeau, but that's a long story. I felt like a kind of spy, and because I was totally ignorant, a lot of people helped me see what I wanted. Ottawa was so full of rumours that for every question I asked, I got at least three answers. The need to find out "the truth" became a theme of the play.

On another level, I surrounded myself with pictures of the Trudeaus. I made two scrapbooks and would spend time simply looking at the pictures and trying to think what was inside those faces. I even did a session with a psychic that involved embodying the characters, and then stepping outside of myself and asking them questions that were puzzling me.

I tried every way I knew to rid myself of past prejudices about either of them. At the end of all this, I had bits and pieces of things written down: ideas for scenes, images, themes, but nothing that resembled a play. Then Paul Thompson and I got together to begin the improvisational "jam session" to create the play.

You were working with two characters. How did Henry arrive?

It developed on a crass level because I was really interested in the character of the journalists I talked to. They had an exotic sense of language. They would say things like, "Look at her, she's beautiful as a Hawaiian flower." They used metaphors a lot and I liked the way they spoke. I liked their sense of interest and their personal connection to political events. What I began to play with was the emotional connection to politics: you fall in love with Trudeau; you fall in love with Canada. Trudeau falls in love with Margaret Sinclair. It's not a logical process. Rather, it comes from a gut level. When people get into arguments and talk politics, it's really emotion talking. It's like arguing about someone's wife — and you can always cheat on your wife, just like you can cheat on the country. I began to see that journalists who had this connection to politics were part of a triangle. In terms of the triangle (if we're making an analogy between love of country and politics), they form the apex. They became involved in politics in Ottawa and they told the country about it. So actually, there's a fourth character in the play: the audience, who represent the people of Canada. And from their point of view, what they watched was the marriage of two people disintegrate. At times, Trudeau even accused the press of having contributed to the problem. They also watched the disintegration of an idealistic relationship between a Prime Minister and his country. And the third party to it all was the journalist who talked about it. There was also the question in my mind as to whether or not the press should have, conscientiously, treated Margaret and Pierre the way they did, while the fourth party, the country, looked on and got as emotionally involved as it did. This summer, in Toronto, a Margaret Trudeau look-alike in a movie was beaten about the head by a woman in the street and when the actress said, "Hey, I'm not Margaret. I'm her look-alike," the woman said, "It doesn't matter," and kept on hitting her.

You've been part of a theatre movement that has taken Canadian mythology and hero-making, if not as its central issue, at least as its dominant theme. How does this play fit in?

I did "If You're So Good, Why Are You in Saskatoon?" where we made heroes out of people who stay in a place that isn't the centre of the country and who love that place, but who are crazy and modern and mixed-up. They're a type of anti-hero. Then I did "Paper Wheat," which was about the total heroism of the ordinary man and about his struggle with nature. Then, I did "Les Maudits Anglais," which was about everyone's stereotyped idea of the Québecois and language difficulties. It really takes a heroic nature to try to understand what this country is all about — because it *is* so complicated. Margaret and Pierre Trudeau are heroes to me, not necessarily conventional hero figures, but in terms of what I was trying to do with the play, making it a metaphor for much larger concerns going on in the ʝuntry and with people, heroes all the same. I find the struggle of any two people trying to stay together heroic. The struggle of a family trying to stay together is heroic, especially in 1980. I find avoiding the inevitability of corruption in politics heroic. I think that there was a real vision in what Trudeau wanted to do. I found a lot of idealism in Ottawa which seemed to be totally thwarted. I found a heroic struggle in the journalists trying to maintain objectivity, while at the same time having to make all kinds of political opinions. It is a heroic struggle for the general public to even try to care about politics, when every effort seems futile. Sometimes I am amazed that people even bother to vote. It's easy to give up and it's easy to disbelieve everything. In this show, I don't proclaim that everything Margaret says is wonderful, nor do I feel that all the political dealings of Pierre have been great. It's not a blanket political statement of support, the play is a metaphor for the country's involvement in politics and love, based on the political and personal realities of two individuals. Maggie and Pierre hold positions as representatives of the people and it satisfied the needs of the people at the time, to watch somebody else's pain and suffering played out in front of them. I like to think of Maggie and Pierre as "epic characters." They are heroes in that they contain all the elements of humanity, magnified. Their story has already been shared by the whole country, and actually, by a lot of the world as well.

I have been told many times, "What right do you have to do a show about the marriage of two living people?" All I can ever think of is that if you asked a minstrel in King Arthur's court what right he had to sing of Guinevere and Lancelot, he would have said, "But that's my best song." I'm aware that a lot of those guys lost their heads. It was once common for art to explore the times through the life of a given ruler. I must be a throwback. Things are going too fast to have to wait for death to tell the story.

Linda Griffiths,
Toronto, Ontario.
September, 1980.

11

SCENES

Act One

1. Henry Doesn't Want To.
2. Tahiti.
3. '68 Convention.
4. Henry's Politician.
5. 17 Magazine.
6. Les Snobs.
7. Grouse Mountain.
8. Pierre Perturbed.
9. Henry's Question.
10. Diplomacy.

Act Two

1. Visions in the Bedroom.
2. October Crisis.
3. Walk Alone.
4. Boredom.
5. Press Club.
6. The Fight.
7. Enter My Emotional World.
8. Disco — Election.
9. Henry's Last Hurrah.

Act One

1. HENRY DOESN'T WANT TO

HENRY IS DISCOVERED ON THE TELEPHONE IN A STATE OF SOME AGITATION. REFUSING A JOB HAS ALWAYS BEEN HARD ON HIM.

HENRY:

No. Absolutely not. That's my final word. I'm not writing about those two any longer. I know what you want. You want exposé, you want the story behind the scenes, you want smut. Well, go on, admit it. Look, I know everything there is to know about those two. I'm just not telling anybody. No, and that's my final word. No.

He hangs up the telephone, begins pacing back and forth and talks to himself.

I'm not writing about those two any longer because I'm not interested. . . . And even if I was interested, I wouldn't write about them. . . for personal reasons. I'm crazy. . . . It'd get picked up right across the country. I'd finally get my byline. . . . No.

15

He turns to the audience.

You see before you a man obsessed, tortured, a walking cliché journalist. . . .except I've heard lately. . . .I don't know if you've heard this. . .that it's a cliché to talk about being a cliché. . .but how else to describe a world still filled with deals, deadlines and the scent of stale election promises in the air? Haunted by two giant figures with two giant pairs of eyes. . . .Maybe if I wrote about them one more time, I'd get them outta my head! Right. . . .No. . . .So what, eh? I mean, so what? So a man marries a woman, they have a couple of kids, they break up, she goes a bit wild, he loses his job, he tries to get it back. So why write about that? What's the difference between them and anybody else? You want to know what the difference is? The one that I figured out anyway. . .that everybody watched. . .millions. . . that close, like voyeurs, or like the circus. . . .Hooray, hooray, hooray. Pierre Trudeau marries twenty-two year old bride. . . .Baby Justin born Christmas Day . . . .Margaret Trudeau hospitalized for nervous breakdown. . . .Pierre Trudeau refuses sympathy election based on separation. . . .Maggie boogies with the Stones and writes exposé book. . . .Joe Clark wins election. . . .Pierre Trudeau resigns as leader of the Opposition, and on and on. You see, I wrote those headlines—me—and because of that and everything that happened, they can never be two small figures to me, like the kind you hold in the palm of your hand. They're huge, they're giants. . . two epic characters, and they carry on a mythological struggle. They're King Arthur and Guinevere, and Clytemnestra and Agamemnon, and they play out our pain way up there. There's something at the centre of the story, something that affected everybody deeper than they're willing to admit. . . .Certainly something that offended everybody! Who's going to tell it but me? Right? Right.

16

He picks up the telephone.

All right, ya son of a bitch, I'm going to do it. . . .
Ya, but my way. What I saw, what I see.

He hangs up.

Funny, it's as if I'd been there at every turn and twist
along the way. . . watching. You know, she was
nineteen years old, and it was one of those bright
white light days in Tahiti, with the waves gently
lapping against the raft. . . .

2. TAHITI

**ON THAT FATEFUL DAY, MARGARET IS
SUNNING HERSELF, CLAD IN A CLASSIC
BATHING SUIT.**

MAGGIE:
I can't believe it. . . . Here I am in Tahiti, at the Club
Méditerranée, I'm getting a half-decent tan, at least
for my kind of skin, and I'm here with my parents.
I don't know what to do with my life. I could open a
school for retarded children, I could join the
Revolution and the Black Panthers. Or just drop out
and do lots of really good drugs. . . . Who's that?
Who's that water skiing? Hey, he's pretty good. Is he
trying to impress me? Of course he is. Men are so
transparent. How old is he? Twenty-five? No, maybe
a little older. I knew it. He's coming over. . . .

PIERRE:
Hello. What's a beautiful girl like you you doing
here all alone?

MAGGIE:

Oh, God. Cutting parental ties, trying to decide what to do with my life. I'm in a state of confusion, but then confusion's the name of the game, so it's all right. What are you doing here?

PIERRE:

I'm reading *The Decline and Fall of the Roman Empire* and deciding whether or not to become Prime Minister of Canada.

MAGGIE:

Sounds really exciting.

PIERRE:

It's not a dull book. You should read about the Bacchanalian rituals.

MAGGIE:

Read about them. I've been there.

PIERRE:

That sounds like a long journey. How much farther do you want to go?

MAGGIE:

Forever. And you?... I want to be world-renowned, to shape destiny, to be deliriously happy. You might say, I want it all.

PIERRE:

I want to be world-renowned, to shape destiny, to be deliriously happy. You might say, I want it all.

MAGGIE:

What did you say?

PIERRE:

> I'm sorry, what did you say?

MAGGIE:

> You heard what I said. Do you mean it?

PIERRE:

> Just watch me.

MAGGIE:

> No. Just watch me.

PIERRE:

> If you're serious about this, I'm sure you'll be interested in exploring the challenges of snorkelling with me tomorrow at ten o'clock.

MAGGIE:

> Maybe.

PIERRE:

> Maybe, you're serious?

MAGGIE:

> Maybe I'll go snorkelling with you, tomorrow at ten o'clock.

> *She exits, having won the day.*

3. '68 CONVENTION

PIERRE APPEARS WAVING TO AN ECSTATIC CROWD. THEY ARE CHANTING, "TRU-DEAU, TRU-DEAU, TRU-DEAU."

PIERRE:

Getting off at the railroad station. . .a spontaneous demonstration, thousands of hands reaching out to touch me, rip off pieces of my clothing, women throwing themselves at my feet. People laughing, crying, kissing, fainting. It's not a leadership campaign, it's more like a coronation!

Cheers are heard.

I wonder how many people have felt this kind of reinforcement, not for their philosophy or ideas, but for their personality, perhaps even for their body. . . .

It's not right, this is the kind of emotionalism that fostered Fascism. I want to tell you that the government is no Santa Claus.

Cheers are heard again.

It's hard to resist. . . . And there will be one Canada and that Canada will be progressive!

Cheers are heard again.

He executes one of his famous pirouettes.

I know what I will do with this Liberal Party. I will take this Right-winger, and this Left-winger and stop all the endless squabbling. I will become like an alchemist and forge out of everyone's opinion, a

shining wheel of a party, a wheel that will go ever
forward, and just a little to the Left.

He exits amid cheers.

4. HENRY'S POLITICIAN

**HENRY ENTERS JUST AS PIERRE LEAVES,
LOOKS AFTER HIM FOR A MOMENT, THEN
ADDRESSES THE AUDIENCE.**

HENRY:
You know, when I first came to Ottawa, I expected it
to be like those TV press conferences, you know the
kind . . . politicians on one side, journalists on the
other and everybody's on the attack. You could
never imagine these people in the same room with
each other. I arrived on Parliament Hill to find a
small town of about 300 people. The doers and the
watchers all mixed in together exchanging
information, drinks and sometimes even wives for
mutual benefit. And I learned the fine lines of
conduct where you can drink with a man one night,
write about him the next and look him right in the
eye the day after. You're never friends and you're
never enemies. Gossip was king, not politics. As for
the rest, we were a pretty boring small town. . . . I
mean, most of the MP's were still staying at the
YMCA. I'd watch Diefenbaker and Pearson hacking
and hewing away at each other like two old gladiators.
The biggest thing that happened was the Flag
Debate. Remember that one? Dief calling on the
old powers of the British Empire only to find out
that they didn't give a shit any longer. We had
nothing going for us except a certain cynical satirical
sense of humour about how ridiculous we were. And

we'd cast those longing glances across the border to you know where.

Then, all of a sudden, out of the clear blue sky, comes this guy. . .and he's sexy and classy and brilliant and athletic and liberal-minded and adventurous! New York was jealous. . .and the bugger spoke French! Guys like that didn't usually dirty their hands with politics. He was a member of the ruling class that chose to rule. We were flattered. And because he was sexy and classy and athletic. . .we became sexy and classy and athletic.

You're from New York, are you? Too bad. . . . Pierre Trudeau? Oh, yeah, just another typical Canadian. French? Sure, most of us are "bilingué parfait." Sexy? Classy? It's the long winters.

And you couldn't understand a goddamn thing the guy was saying. . . . Rows of journalists down at the library. . . . Who the hell is Loqueville? Or is it Toqueville? Has anyone read *Buddhism and the Natural Man*? It was fantastic. I loved the guy.

And all the while I was watching him, enjoying him, I had this almost eerie sensation that things were going to get unusually complicated. . .I just didn't know how!

5. 17 MAGAZINE

MARGARET IS PENSIVE IN HER GOOD GIRL DRESS. AT FIRST, SHE IS REMOVED, AS IF TELLING SOMEONE ELSE'S STORY. LATER, SHE BECOMES MORE DESPERATE TO BE WHERE "IT'S HAPPENING."

MAGGIE:

It wasn't as if she was timid or afraid, it was as if, as she went towards what was expected, she went just a little bit too far, beyond the delicate point of naturalness, giving everything she did and said a strange air of falsity that she herself questioned at every turn.

VOICE:

Margaret. You're trying just a bit too hard.

MAGGIE:

No, it's what they want. . . . Hello, Daddy. I've got your pipe and slippers. Hello, Mr. Jenkins. Daddy, is it all right if I sit on Mr. Jenkins' lap? I'm glad you think I'm pretty as a picture. I have to go now to meet the captain of the football team. . . . I. . . .

VOICE:

Margaret, look around. No one else is dating the captain of the football team.

MAGGIE:

No one else is still acting like me. No one else is still dressed like me.

Her dress comes apart and drops to her knees. She heaves a sigh of relief.

VOICE:
>Margaret, put on your blue jeans.

MAGGIE:
>I don't think I like these kind of clothes. I like things with a bit of lace on them. . . . Ohhhhh, I understand. Oh, yeah. . . . They're for sitting on the ground with your legs open wide, they're for. . . *Chanting*. . . . "We're not going to class, we're not going to class". . . They're for. . . *Singing*. . . . "There is a house in New Orleans, they call the rising sun . . . ."

VOICE:
>Margaret. . . look around.

MAGGIE:
>Where'd everybody go?

VOICE:
>Late again, Margaret. No one goes to university anymore. They've all gone to Exotica, to Greece and Africa.

MAGGIE:
>All right, I'll go too. I'll lose my middle class cleanliness there. . . .

VOICE:
>How are you going to get there?

MAGGIE:
>With $2,000.00 worth of Dad's money, but I'm not going to spend it. . . . It's off to Morocco and Marakesh, really strange food and really strange dope.

VOICE:
>Margaret, you still sound like a phony.

MAGGIE:

I'm trying. . . . Living a communal existence where
you pretend you don't need any privacy at all. Of
course, I'll make love to you, I'm not afraid of my
body. You're not afraid of yours and I'll even enjoy
it, and I'll make love to you and you and you and
you. . . . Standing in a gold-domed square with some
guy going, "Nyahhhhhhhhh. . . ." How come all of a
sudden everybody looks like something out of a Bible
School picture? How come they think I'm the Virgin
Mary? And what's worse, how come I think I'm the
Virgin Mary? This is too freaky, too weird. . . .
Back to B.C. and Canada . . . Granny's cabin in the
woods. . . .

VOICE:

Margaret . . . you're not even a real hippie, you're just
thinking about what a pretty picture you make
wandering around the trees.

MAGGIE:

First, what's a real hippie? Second, yes, I am
thinking about that, but I'm thinking on the inside
too. You can be outside and inside at the same time,
you know. . . .

VOICE:

Answer the telephone.

MAGGIE:

Mom? How did you find me? . . . Heyyyyy, get real, I
don't go out on dates anymore. . . . Who? Pierre
Trudeau? That's for real!

6. LES SNOBS

PIERRE SPEAKS AS THOUGH DISCOVERING THIS PERSON HIMSELF, ALMOST SURPRISED AT HIS OWN ACTIONS, PHYSICALIZING EVERY STEP ALONG THE WAY. HE BEGINS BY ZIPPING UP A BLACK LEATHER JACKET.

PIERRE:

Imagine a man, no, a child, about three years old
and his parents are telling him to go to bed, and he
says, "No, you're wrong." Why? "Because the book
I'm reading now is more important to my future
development than the fifteen minutes more you want
me to sleep." Imagine him then seeing that look on
his parents' faces of unquestioning authority. . . .
I'm right because I'm right because I'm right. . . .
And imagine him resolving, for the rest of his days,
to fight that look. Five years old, hearing somewhere
that fresh air is good for you, up goes the window.

He begins to deep breathe.

Six years old, the 5-BX plan, self-discipline, twenty
minutes every day. Why? To be strong. What for?
To fight. Who? I don't know yet, but I'm going to
find out very soon. . . .

Sitting in the classroom . . . the Battle of the Plains of
Abraham. The students are looking maudlin, the
teacher's getting out her handkerchief and there's
a general air of cloying sentimentality in the room.
"And so, Montcalm lost his life, Québec lost her
heart, and we went down the drain to the dastardly
English." Hurrah for the English!!! You should have
seen the look on their faces. . . . What are we talking
about? Winners? Losers? If we had won, would we
not be cheering for ourselves? Who fought the best

battle? The English. We deserved to lose. We'll always lose, so long as we drown in waves of emotionalism. "Don't think, Pierre, just feel?" Exactly! If thought is an enemy, then we are Fascists!...I've never known if I say these things because I really believe them or because I just like bugging people....

Brébeuf College, becoming a member of an élite group called, "Les Snobs"....Enemies of righteousness. We dress up in German uniforms during World War II, knock on people's doors and tell them they've been arrested. Why? To make them examine their own sense of safety....

Sick of Québec, sick of empty nationalist whining, off to Harvard Law School, and it's Law and Society and Man. How does it all fit together? And where do I fit in? Maybe Paris, the Sorbonne, my attic apartment, my Mercedes downstairs, six o'clock in the morning, a freezing cold room, a basin of ice water...all down a naked body. Why? To be strong. What for? To fight. Who? First myself, and then... anyone who dares me....

Off to find adventure, danger, the War Zones... China, Vietnam, Palestine. I get arrested. Why? To find out what it's like. And then, it's the internal journey of the soul, and so it's Buddhism and chanting and yoga. All right, body, soul, mind, all tuned, all tingling....

Come on.... What don't I know? Come on.... Québec? I'm always thinking of Québec. A dictatorship to fight? We are our own dictators. You dare me? So, it's back to Québec, the Asbestos Strike, thousands of cheering workers...."It is the time to take up arms against the oppressors; now is the time for cataclysms!" Practical politics, Pelletier's kitchen . . . Lévesque, Marchand, Pelletier. What about Québec? What about Federalism? Where do we fit in, where are we going wrong? Writing treatises against the Liberal Party. They're only interested in perpetuating their own power, it has no . . . . Come to Ottawa? You've got to be kidding? The Liberal Party? I don't think they would take me. They will? A challenge is a challenge. Why not?

7. GROUSE MOUNTAIN

MARGARET IS BEHIND A SCREEN, RUSHING THROUGH THE MOTIONS OF PREPARING FOR A DATE. THE ABSURDITY OF THE SITUATION IS BEGINNING TO DAWN ON HER.

MAGGIE:

Oh, no! I look like a Barbie Doll. Why did I let them do that to my hair? Cheryl, will you bring up that stuff . . . . All this fuss, for what? Just another corrupt politician. I was even going to put that junk on my nails. I can't believe it. I gave up all this materialistic crap a long time ago, matching handbags, high-heeled . . . shoes.

A moment of appreciation, quickly squashed.

Look at this dress, we could have lived for six months in Morocco for what this cost. It's immoral.

She struggles with the dress, then stands with it over her head and laughs.

It's like a viewfinder made of lace.

The dress slips down over her head and she looks at herself in an imaginary mirror.

I don't know why I'm so nervous, I guess if I want to, I can look all right....

Don't answer the doorbell. And cool the giggling, all right?

She opens the door.

He's so little, he's just a little taller than me. I can't look at him. Oh, no, he's offering me his arm. Thank you. You're wearing a cravat! Oh, no, I just don't know anybody that wears cravats.... And a month ago in Morocco, we weren't wearing anything at all. Oh, great, it's the kind of restaurant my parents go to. No, no, that's fine. He's pushing my chair in, I hope I don't land on my ass.... Thank you. I'm pressing my knees together so hard my thighs hurt. What did I take in university? Political Science, I took Politi.... Bad choice, Margaret. Did you really win a contest for having the most beautiful legs in the world?... He thinks I'm an idiot. How strange, it's as if I'm falling into his eyes.... 100% charm and all real. He's trying to tell me something... that he's shy too! It's as if every word I say is a jewel!... It's like he's massaging me from the inside! I can tell you anything. What were my courses like in university? Well, Pierre, they're about a whole generation of people just stepping back and saying, "Hey, hold on." They're about people looking at war and money and corruption and politics and saying, "Look, there's got to be a better way." About everybody feeling a part of a whole movement, going, "Don't trust anyone over thirty!!!"

She realizes she's put her foot in it.

Basically, Pierre, I just do really a lot of dope . . . .
He's laughing. He's not shocked at all. He likes me
talking like this. Is he an old man or what? . . .

Flash, flash, flash . . . . Autograph hunters . . . .

Margaret Sinclair. No, that's all right, you can take
my picture. Oh, God, I hope I look all right . . . .

Flash, flash, flash, flash . . . .

Funny, signing those autographs, he looked like
Clark Gable. And a while back, talking politics, he
reminded me of that guy with the khaki shorts that
used to follow me around Morocco. And just then,
ordering the wine, he looked like Ricardo
Montalban. He changes, frame to frame to frame.
It's like watching television! He's making a funny,
little old-fashioned bow that matches the cravat. It's
so cute. He's asking me to dance. "Of course, I'll
dance with you . . . ."

> *They dance to a ballad by Margaret's favourite
> rock and roll band.*

Do you know what this reminds me of? One night
when I was thirteen years old, my mother and father
and I went down to the rec room, and my mother
played the record player and my father taught me to
dance. Dancing with you is like dancing with my
father.

PIERRE:
You're making me feel old.

37

MAGGIE:

I'm sorry. You could never be old.

PIERRE:

I'm two years older than your mother.

MAGGIE:

You'll never be old. . . . I can feel his body underneath the suit. Strong, but not like a football player's. Flexible, like a dancer's.

She giggles.

PIERRE:

What are you laughing at?

MAGGIE:

Oh, I'm just not used to dancing this way.

PIERRE:

You intimidate me when you laugh.

MAGGIE:

I intimidate the Prime Minister of Canada! Hey, you wouldn't be intimidated by a string of Mack trucks.

PIERRE:

You have soft hair.

MAGGIE:

He thinks I have soft hair. . . . How much do I want? Don't blow it, Margaret, just open your eyes wide and make him think of hyacinths. It's like flowers in springtime and every atom in my body feeling alive. . . . No, exploding. . . . It's like really good acid and being on mescaline for eight hours and sitting

up in a tree, thinking you're a bird. . . . Come on
Pierre, baby, let's dance all night!

PIERRE:

Margaret? Don't you think we should be going?
Everyone's left.

MAGGIE:

I didn't even notice. Isn't that a line out of some
movie?

PIERRE:

I don't know. I don't often go to movies.

MAGGIE:

Are you going to take me right home?

PIERRE:

I'm a well-brought up boy, I get my eight hours
sleep. I have a busy day tomorrow. Yes, I suppose so.

MAGGIE:

I mean. . . where are you staying?

PIERRE:

At the nearest CP Hotel. . . . It's Canadian. . . . It's a
joke. . . .

MAGGIE:

Far-out, Pierre. That's really good. Well, I guess it's
goodnight.

PIERRE:

Come and see me if you ever get to Ottawa. I'd be
interested to see what happens to you. Give me a
call. We'll have dinner. Thank you for an
enchanting evening.

They kiss and PIERRE exits, leaving
MARGARET with a last thought, as the
music swells.

MAGGIE:
>   It's like . . . kissing a dried rose.

8. PIERRE PERTURBED

**PIERRE AND HENRY ARE IN A MURKY BAR.
BOTH ARE SLIGHTLY UNCOMFORTABLE,
AWARE OF THE UNUSUALNESS OF THEIR
SITUATION.**

PIERRE:
>   Well, Henry, you're probably wondering why I've
>   brought you here to this out-of-the-way bar, in this
>   out-of-the-way part of Ottawa.

HENRY:
>   Yeah, yeah, to tell you the truth, I had been
>   wondering why you brought me here, seeing as how
>   I've only spoken with you about twice.

PIERRE:
>   You seem to be a man of some discretion . . . have
>   experience in certain areas, and I was in need of
>   advice in a hurry . . . and you were available. A
>   personal matter. Three triple Scotches, please.

HENRY:
>   But you don't drink . . . . All right, if you're in need of
>   a little advice, sir, go right ahead. Believe me, I'm
>   all ears.

PIERRE:

I'm thinking of marrying a twenty-two year old flower child.

HENRY:

Is she pretty?

PIERRE:

Don't be banal.

HENRY:

Don't you have someone else you can talk to, like a friend?

PIERRE:

No.

HENRY:

Sorry. . . . How do you feel about her, or something like that? I don't know.

PIERRE:

I don't know, I'm completely confused. I'm wandering around Ottawa in a kind of a daze. I keep thinking of flowers, but I can't remember what kind. I walk into Parliament and sit there facing Bob Stanfield, and last week, he and the entire Conservative Party transformed into Margaret. I don't know, I think perhaps, that it is time for me to embark on the ultimate relationship between a man and a woman — "I WANT A WIFE" — the sharing of a lifetime. . . . I see little children playing in the street, and I think, I love children — "I WANT SONS" — and daughters. I feel experiences welling up inside of me such as I've never felt before — "I WANT SOMEONE TO FUCK ME SILLY" — I don't know, I'm baffled, I'm bewildered. . . . I think I'm smitten.

HENRY:
When guys like you fall, they really go, don't they,
Pierre? Sorry, not funny. All right, you want to
know what I think? Man to man, and not Prime
Minister to journalist? I think it's a really stupid
idea. Look, most of the women in the country vote
for you because they think you're going to come
through the bedroom window one night. I mean,
think of all the votes!. . . Show me one of these May-
to-September things that has ever worked out, just
one. You got to watch yourself. She followed you to
Ottawa, she's out to trap you. You can't trust a
woman like that. Treat her like you treat the
Cabinet. . . . I think you should get up, go over to
that telephone and tell the dolly, "No go". . . sir.

PIERRE:
Of course, you're right. This is a crisis and I'm
always good in a crisis. Thank you. . . .

He picks up the telephone.

Margaret? Yes, I have been thinking about you. Yes,
I do remember, it was wonderful. . . . I wanted to
discuss this entire marriage question with you. . . .
What do you mean, "When?" No, you don't
understand, I mean, the dialogue must be completely
revamped. "What kind of ring do I want?". . . No,
no, you don't understand, March is a terrible time
for me. . . . What about February?

He realizes what he's just said.

All right, what about February?

*He hangs up the telephone with an air of rueful
resignation. The lights fade to black.*

9. HENRY'S QUESTION

HENRY BECOMES A GREEK MESSENGER, DESCRIBING WHAT IS INVISIBLE TO THE AUDIENCE BY PEEKING BEHIND A CURTAIN, WHERE THE TWO CHARACTERS, UNAWARE, ARE CONTINUING THEIR TETE A TETE.

HENRY:

Have . . . have you ever been involved in a key turning point in somebody else's life, you know what I mean? And forever after, no matter what else happens, you always feel involved? Well, that's what happened to me. I mean, it just doesn't make sense. . . . Out of all the women that man could have had, why this one? I gotta find out. . . .

So they're back at that restaurant, right? . . . Right. It's her I have to see. Hold on. . . .

He looks behind the curtain.

She's beautiful as a Hawaiian flower . . . and she's a kook. That's it! He's afraid of becoming one of those grey-faced zombies that wander around Ottawa. She's supposed to balance the act. But the poor kid. Look at him. . . .

He peeks again.

Oh, God! He's using every move in the book on her. It's a route. "Why don't you pick on someone your own size, Trudeau?" She doesn't want to be a rose in his lapel.

He looks at her.

Oh, yes, she does! She's bringing out a few moves of her own. She's bringing out the old feminine wiles. "Watch out, Trudeau, this woman's dangerous!" She's using her youth against his age — no — he's using his age against her youth. . . . They're doing it to each other. . . . No, there's got to be a bad guy and there's got to be a victim. . . .

He throws open the curtains and is about to interfere. . . .

"Sorry. . .sorry. . .I. . .I didn't understand." I mean, sensitivity is not exactly my strong point. But, if you don't believe in that, what do you believe in?

10. DIPLOMACY

MARGARET IS DRESSING UP AGAIN, BUT THIS TIME IT IS MORE NATURAL TO HER. THIS IS HER FIRST MAJOR SOCIAL EVENT AS WIFE OF THE PRIME MINISTER AND SHE SEES THE POSSIBILITY FOR EVANGELISM IN HER NEW ROLE.

MAGGIE:
Remember, you belong to the richest, healthiest, best-educated generation ever to hit the face of the earth, and there are millions of you. You're the first one of your kind ever to brave the bastion of their world. They're going to ask a lot of questions about what's been going on. Answer them all, be open, be vulnerable, don't let them get to you. . . . Show them what a little love is all about. Remember, you're walking in there on the arm of the Prime Minister of Canada. . . . You got him and they didn't. . . .

The Governor-General's Ball. It's like the high school prom, except everybody's older. The world is run by Mums and Dads, in their rented tuxedos and one long dress.

To PIERRE.

Don't worry, I'll be fine. I'll dance with you later . . . .

Hiiii . . . . How are you? Do you know what it's like to be at a rock concert with 15,000 people, and everybody's thinking the same thing . . . that some kind of change is bound to . . . happen.

Her conversation partner drifts away, uncomprehending, and she tries again.

Yeah, oh . . . . Oh . . . . Thank you . . . . Oh . . . . you're very kind . . . . Thank you . . . .

Hiiii . . . . How are you? Look, I know what happened to your son. He started to grow his hair long, didn't want to be a doctor, and told you to fuck off. Look, I know where that's coming from. I can help you. Just . . . . You think that everyone who smokes dope should be shot! . . . You're in Pierre's Cabinet?!?!?!

She runs to PIERRE and they dance.

MAGGIE:
Pierre, it's almost insulting. They . . . they think I'm one of them. They don't even see the difference.

PIERRE:
You can't change everything in a single night. Just be yourself, just be natural.

MAGGIE:
Why don't they realize they're obsolete?

PIERRE:
Maybe they think you're obsolete.

MAGGIE:

She begins greeting Heads of State.

MAGGIE:
Mr. Chairman Mao, how do you do? Mr. Chou-En-Lai. . . .

Bowing a little uncertainly.

It's a pleasure, sir.

With confidence.

Mr. Kosygin. Mr. Nixon. . . .

A moment of recognition.

Mr. Nixon. Queen Elizabeth. . . .

She falls while curtsying.

Queen Elizabeth! Prince Charles. . . .

A subtle gesture to the neck of her gown.

Prince Charles! Fidel Castro. . . . Hi! . . .

Mr. Brezhnev, you know I went to Russia, and what bothered me about Communism was the uniformity that I saw.

The lights dim and she hears distant rock
music. It fades away. The lights come up abruptly.
Her manner is now nervous and strained, overly
formal.

I think that both our countries have really a lot to say
to each other because they're both . . . cold. . . .

Mrs. Meir, I wanted to go to Israel on my travels, but
there was a war going on. I mean, people were
dying. You're a leader, can't you do something. . . .

The lights dim. The music returns, slightly
louder this time. She loses herself in the music,
her hips swaying in appreciation. The music
fades. The lights come up. She searches for
small talk.

Ohh, you know babies, they'll come along when they
want to come along. . . . Yeah, yeah. . . .

Mr. Nixon, do you have any idea what you represent
to the people of my generation!? To everybody!?
You're a symbol of evil, of corruption. I know people
that want to shoot. . . .

The music returns, even more compellingly.
She begins to dance. The music stops and she is
shocked into reality.

How are Pat and . . . Trish? . . .

The music returns again. She is lost in the
sound of Sixties' electric guitars. She dances
wildly, then recovers. The music swells over her
exit line.

I'd like to tell you how much I've enjoyed meeting you all and how much I look forward to seeing you again in the near future.

Act Two

1. VISIONS IN THE BEDROOM

MARGARET AND PIERRE LOLLING AROUND, LETTING THEIR MINDS WANDER FREELY TOWARDS PHILOSOPHY AND THE WAYS OF THE WORLD.

MAGGIE:
> So now you have me, and the country, and everybody's rooting for you, what are you going to do with the "all" that you've got?

PIERRE:
> I'm going to lead us all into the Golden Age.

MAGGIE:
> Are you suffering from delusions of grandeur? Come on, it sounds as if you really believed in "The Just Society" or something. Look, I've been around enough politicians. It's okay to say something just to get in. Oh, no. . . . Oh, no, you do, you really believe it.

PIERRE:

Here's the voice of youth, of optimism, a true
daughter of the age of Aquarius. Margaret, of
course I believe in it, it only makes sense. Why do
they just want to touch me? Why is the whole country
at my feet? Because I'm the first guy that ever walked
into the House of Commons of this country with an
idea . . . of how a whole society should work.
Discussion, philosophy and idealism creating a new
order. We are on the threshold of a model of
harmony and vitality for the world. Emmanuel
Mounier writes of Creative Democracy. If we could
only just believe in the possibility.

MAGGIE:

But you're talking about Ottawa. Ottawa's full of
frumps, they'd never understand what you were
saying. I'm sorry, I know, you mean . . . change or
the Revolution. Sure, I believe in it. I know lots of
people that do. Sure, I have a vision of a world, but
it's not practical. Sometimes early in the morning, I
can see it so clear. I see a wood, and sunlight
streaming down, and people dancing naked like
fauns, dappled sunshine on their bodies, fearless . . .
but I don't know where they pay their taxes, or get
their pay cheques. But you know something about
those people? They're totally free.

PIERRE:

Well, all right, maybe there's a place for that in
"The Just Society." Maybe on sunny days, I should
walk into Parliament and say, "Everybody out, all
the MP's walk along the Ottawa River, take off your
clothes, jump in and make love to your wives, or your
girlfriends or someone." Just think how it would
change the face of government. . . . I want to know
what happens if you put a Communist, a Socialist
and some guy from the Canadian Legion together in

the same room and you make them fight it
out. . . . And you are the irrationality that perhaps
somewhere along the line I have lost. You are the
jolt of electricity that will set the whole thing going
like some kind of ecstatic merry-go-round.

MAGGIE:

I don't know. . . . Why don't you call it something
like, "The Psychedelic, Nutso, Let-It-All-Hang-Out
Society."

PIERRE:

You're being silly. It's "The Reasonable, Yet
Tolerant Society."

MAGGIE:

You can't tolerate freedom!

PIERRE:

All right. All right. Then it's "The Reasonable, Yet
Impulsive Just Society."

MAGGIE:

I'm still a bit worried, and I think if you want to
keep your little jolt of electricity, you'll have to chase
your wife, outside, and we're gonna have to. . . DO
IT IN THE ROAD!

She disappears, laughing.

2. OCTOBER CRISIS

HENRY CATCHES PIERRE OUTSIDE THE PARLIAMENT BUILDINGS. HE AND HIS TAPE RECORDER ARE WORRIED ABOUT FREEDOM.

HENRY:
Sir, sir . . . . What are all these guys with all these guns running around?

PIERRE:
Haven't you noticed?

HENRY:
Yeah, I noticed. I wondered why you people decided to have them?

PIERRE:
Well, what's your worry?

HENRY:
I'm not worried, but you seem to be.

PIERRE:
If you're not worried, then I'm not worried.

HENRY:
All right, I'm worried. I'm worried about living in a society where you have to resort to that kind of thing.

PIERRE:
It seems natural that if people are going to be abducted, we should take steps to protect them. What would you do if another Minister were to be abducted?

HENRY:
    Well, that isn't the. . . .

PIERRE:
    Is it your position that we should give in to the seven
    demands of the FLQ?

HENRY:
    No. That is not my position at all.

PIERRE:
    What is your position?

HENRY:
    My position is you don't give in to any of them.

PIERRE:
    But you don't protect yourself against the possibility
    of blackmail?

HENRY:
    Well, how can you protect everybody, without
    turning the place into a Police State?

PIERRE:
    You can't. But are you therefore suggesting we
    should protect no one?

        He is confused, then rallies.

HENRY:
    Right.

PIERRE:
    That's your position?

HENRY:

Right...sir. Sir, sir....Sir, all right, maybe I
explained it badly, but what you're talking about to
me is choices, and my choice is to live in a society
that's free and democratic, and that means you don't
have guys with guns running around in it.

PIERRE:

Correct.

HENRY:

And that means I might have to take the chance
that a guy like you may be abducted.

PIERRE:

Precisely. But I consider it more important to
protect a democratically elected government,
despite the protests of a few weak-kneed, bleeding
hearts, who just don't like the look of a few guns. As
far as I'm concerned, they can just go on and bleed.

HENRY:

How far are you willing to go with that?

PIERRE:

Just watch me!

3. WALK ALONE

RAIN IS FALLING AND MARGARET IS TRYING TO DEAL WITH THE SERVANTS. SHE WANTS TO RID HERSELF OF THE FEELING SHE IS BEING FOLLOWED.

MAGGIE:

Mrs. Trudeau is being difficult today. No, no, I don't want to wear my galoshes. No, thank you, I don't want a rain hat or an umbrella. Don't you understand? I'm from B.C. We like the rain. I just want to go for a walk by my. . . .

She sees the Security Guards who will accompany her.

Oh, no, those guys don't have to come, do they?. . . Mrs. Trudeau is being difficult today, always a scene. . . . Rain on my face, soaking through my clothes. These Easterners will never understand. Oh, no, one of them slipped! There's a place I like, down by the river, where the sewage dumps in. It looks like a waterfall. There's 24 Sussex Drive, way up on the cliff. They're watching me from the windows. And there's the spiral of a church we don't even go to, and there are the Parliament Buildings, where he is. Funny, there's a kind of smoke that comes out of those chimneys coloured like faerie dust. Sometimes it's red and sometimes it's blue and sometimes it's gold. That's when he's talking. Political dust, and pretty soon, it gets all over you and you've got an axe to grind or a position to defend. Hey! Hey, what's that? What's that movement on the water? It looks like wings, like wings beating underneath the water. Pierre would say, "No, Margaret. It's just the intersection of the wind and the rain causing that configuration on the surface." But I know it's wings.

Is it possible to think if someone is always watching you?

> *She runs, hides and comes back. Then, she speaks to the Guards.*

Sorry, I just wanted to hide. I just wanted to hide. They have no idea of what that means....Do I? Someone new watching, a new maid....Oh, boy. No. It's me. It's me....Watching Mrs. Trudeau standing just a little bit close to the water. It's me, all dressed up in my Yves St. Laurent gown, a monument to good taste. It's me watching me, down by the river, a monument to bad taste. She wants me up there....She's beckoning....

> *Silently, she mouthes the words....*

No way....

4. BOREDOM

THE MASTER AND MISTRESS OF 24 SUSSEX DRIVE TRY TO MAKE IT WORK.

PIERRE:
Margaret, I'm home. As Heraclites said, "You never walk in the same river twice," and that's what being Prime Minister of Canada is like. The only way to stay alive is to avoid their wish to define you. Am I a millionaire who's never worked a day in his life, or a dangerous Communist? Québecois or a sellout? They'll never find out. I'm even enjoying the process of their disillusionment in me. How perfect it is! The very things they loved of me six years ago, they can't stand in me now. I think

what irritates them is the sight of a guy having a good time being Prime Minister. How I love it!

MAGGIE:

I just got bored, just this moment. A frozen moment in time. Boredom came crashing through the ceiling and landed right there on the carpet like a piece of rotting meat. What am I doing with this man? We have nothing to say to each other . . . .

All the doors just opened, hundreds and thousands of them, the sunlight streaming through. Nothing is certain, anything is possible. I could be a journalist or an actress . . . .

PIERRE:

Margaret, what's going on?

MAGGIE:

All the doors just opened!

PIERRE:

Congratulations! I've been waiting for this moment to happen to you, when you stand there, full of self-confidence, and you watch all those possibilities open up. And you say, "I'll take a bit of this, a bit of that." Experience it to the end of your synapse. It's a wonderful feeling.

MAGGIE:

I could be a nuclear scientist.

PIERRE:

Of course, you could be a nuclear scientist.

MAGGIE:

Or a rock singer. I could sing like Tina Turner.

PIERRE:
Who?

MAGGIE:
Tina Turner. She's a rock singer, Pierre. But I don't
know, the light is blinding me. . . .

"Bee-bop, Bee-bop-a-doo — Attica, Attica — Make
Love, Not War — Freedom's just another word for
nothing left to lose — Love is never having to say
you're sorry — Freedom Is, Freedom Is — Drop-in,
Drop-out — Speed Kills — One Flew over the Cuckoo's
Nest into the Psychedelic Sunset — Spaceship Earth,
take-off — Timothy Leary, where are you
now? — Sing it, Janice — Ball and Chain — I lost my
ball and chain — I knew it was around here
somewhere — You know what I mean, Jellybean?"

PIERRE:
Margaret, are you all right?

MAGGIE:
No, I'm freaking out. I think there's one thing with
all your knowledge, that you've never understood . . .
human frailty.

PIERRE:
You're right. I don't understand what it's like to live
on your kind of edge. I have never freaked out . . .
but I'm trying. I love you. And after those brown
boxes full of important papers take me away, we
could raid the kitchen for caviar or watch a late
movie . . . "The Wild Bandit of Borneo" is on. You
like that sort of thing.

He kisses her and leaves.

MAGGIE:
>"Sometimes I feel like a motherless child. . . .
> Sometimes I feel like a motherless child. . . .
> Sometimes I feel like a motherless child. . . .
> A long way from home, a long way from home."

> *As she sings each line of the song, another*
> *child wants to sit on her knee, until finally, all*
> *three of her children are balanced with*
> *difficulty. The lights fade.*

5. PRESS CLUB

HENRY AND MARGARET ARE FOUND IN THE JOURNALIST'S HANG-OUT (BAR) ACROSS THE STREET FROM THE PEACE TOWER. THEY HAVE MET IN THE STREET BY CHANCE.

HENRY:
I still haven't figured out how you managed to drag me in here to get drunk with you at the Press Club of all places. I was walking along, minding my own business. . . .

MAGGIE:
Henry, you said you wanted to get drunk.

HENRY:
But not with the Prime Minister's wife!

MAGGIE:
Come on, it was okay to have a couple of drinks with you boys on the campaign plane and on the trip to Cuba. . . . Who am I going to hang loose with, Mrs. Michener? You always seem to have such a high time here.

HENRY:

Yeah, it's a ball. All right, all right, it's not as if we were hiding you or anything. The last time I saw you was at that dinner where you dropped mashed potatoes all down your . . . .

MAGGIE:

And you wrote about it. How is it you always remember these little details so clearly?

HENRY:

I'm a good reporter . . . . All right, all right, let's get the show on the road here. You know most of the journalists. Go right ahead, it's your night . . . .

MAGGIE:

Hii. Oh, hiii. Good to see you . . . . Oh, you know, pre-natal . . . post-natal depression, it's either one or the other with me . . . . Politics! Oh, God, I hate politics! . . . I just keep telling him I wish he'd lose the next election . . . .

HENRY:

Margaret, Margaret, Margaret! . . . No, forget it, it's your night, go ahead . . . .

MAGGIE:

Ah, no, there's no trouble with that. Come on, he's got the body of a twenty-five year old . . . . He does! Look, our sex life is great. Sometimes I dress up in this little garter belt and . . . .

HENRY:

Margaret, Margaret! There's a limit to "off the record."

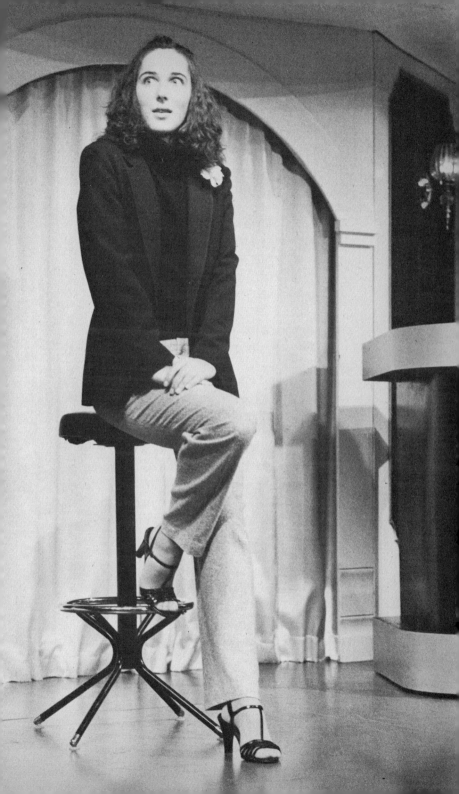

MAGGIE:
I've known these people for years, aren't they my friends?

HENRY:
No.

MAGGIE:
I know what you're talking about.

> *She breaks into a mimed relationship with the camera. At first, it has a mind of its own, viewing her at its own whim. Finally, she wrenches the focus back to herself with a vengeance.*

Those cameras, always on me. At first, I was really nervous, all those stupid pictures of me with that grin and...."I'm very happy to be married to the Prime Minister of Canada." And then, they'd go away and I'd relax. And back again...."I'd like to tell you something about the man you may be voting for. He's not cold and he's not unfeeling. As a matter of fact, he's taught me a lot about loving.... No, I wasn't in the hospital for a cold or something. I'm under severe emotional stress and psychiatric care, and I think that anyone else in that position should tell people and break the taboos.

> *She sings.*

"Mrs. Perez, you are working hard,
    with loving arms,
  Mrs. Perez, both you and I know,
    this is the shittiest job in the world,
  Mrs....."

72

Naked on the beach. . . . That's a funny question to ask, but I'll answer it. The trouble is, my nipples. . . . Have you ever breast-fed three children? No, eh? Well, your nipples go all brown and sticky on the edges. . . . What do you want?

HENRY:

Margaret, Margaret, Margaret! Whoa, whoa, whoa! Is that what *you* want? Haven't you figured this out yet? This is the snake pit. Don't trust them. Especially, don't trust me. I don't know why, but you're news, front page, just like your husband. You have got to watch out. The guy that interviews you has got to be his own censor. You'll say anything. It's frightening. Here, let me tell you a story. One day, I'm down in the library looking up some goddamn thing your husband said, something about Erasmus, and I come across Erasmus' letter to a young man going to court. It has advice in it like, "Confide in no one, yet seem to confide in all, never lower your position or become familiar, or you'll be hated for it." That's it, you're in court. Everybody gets weird when they talk about people in power. Do you have any idea what they're saying out there? That Trudeau screws R.C.M.P. officers under the bed, that you get off on it, that your kids were artificially inseminated. . . . I'm telling you, this gets heavy, watch out!

> *PIERRE enters.*

PIERRE:

Margaret, I just received a call from my Press Secretary. I think it's time we were going home.

73

MAGGIE:

Oh, just a few more minutes. Come on, I'm humanizing your image, and believe me, it needs to be humanized. It's okay, Henry is taking good care of me.

HENRY:

Yeah. It's all right, sir. I'm keeping an eye on her. Don't worry about a thing.

PIERRE:

You're keeping an eye on her? You'll exploit a fine person who happens to trust you. She'll speak freely to you, you'll write it down, she'll look like a fool, and you'll make money off her.

MAGGIE:

No. That's not what he meant at all . . . .

HENRY:

No, no. It's all right, Marg, you don't have to defend me. It's just your husband's usual position on journalists. I think it's about time you realized, sir, that you've been better treated by the journalists of this country than any leader in the Western World.

PIERRE:

Margaret, I'm really not interested in a scene, the car is waiting.

MAGGIE:

I know this sounds terrible, but it's getting exciting and I want to know what happens.

HENRY:
Your wife was starting to look forty-five years old.
Tonight, look at her. Her eyes are glowing, her
cheeks are pink, she's starting to look very...good.
Just let the lady have a good time, will you?

PIERRE:
Margaret, you're my wife and we're going home.

HENRY:
Aha! I knew it. You're a Dictator in the House and a
dictator in the house. Let me tell you something. I
don't like the way you treat your wife, I don't like the
way you treat journalists, and I don't like the way
you treat the country.

MAGGIE:
Hey...what are you fighting about? I like the way
both of you treat me.

PIERRE:
Speaking of the country...if I make a mistake, I'm
responsible to twenty-two million people. Who are
you responsible to? I speak issues and you write
personality. And if arrogance sells newspapers, then
I'm arrogant. You're not a political analyst, you are
paid to make me look like a fool, and I'm sorry, I
don't enjoy being made to look like a fool.

MAGGIE:
Stop fighting. You're making me like it.

HENRY:

And who am I to criticize the great Pierre Elliott Trudeau? Just some poor schmuck off the street. You're the guy that's making a whole country feel stupid. You're giving us a worse inferiority complex than we had before. Now, we feel inferior to you.... You betrayed me! You betrayed all of us. You made us believe that some change was going to happen within the system, and then, you shattered it. And that's why we're out to get you, because you personally betrayed me, personally.

MAGGIE:

Henry, you're acting like a betrayed lover. Don't you understand? I'm the lover here.

PIERRE:

And I'm the one betrayed. I came in here with new ideas all laid out. There was O.F.Y. and L.I.P. and Information Canada. A latticework throughout the country for people to take hold and start believing in their own democracy. But I went a bit slow for you. You got scared and you retreated to your official position—"All politicians are crooks, they're just in it for another vote, they're trying to put one over on you." And you undermined the very basis of my credibility. You weakened the country I was trying to strengthen.

HENRY:

No, you became corrupt. You.... Elitist!

PIERRE:

You Barbarian!

HENRY:

You condescending, arrogant prig!

PIERRE:

> You dark vestige of a Neanderthal Age!...
> Margaret, it's time to go.

MAGGIE:

> I think Henry's a little bit upset. Why don't you just
> let me talk to him by myself for a minute? You can
> just wait in the car. Okay?

> *PIERRE leaves.*

MAGGIE:

> Henry, men are so funny when they fight. Why
> aren't you supposed to talk about politics, religion,
> or sex? Because they're all the same thing. You're not
> going to print anything that happened tonight, are
> you?

HENRY:

> Margaret, is it possible that you're not as naive as I
> think you are? Are you trying to pull my strings? Is it
> conceivable that you are trying to get somewhere?
> Are you capable of ambition? Why am I in love with
> you? Why does the whole Press Gallery have fantasies
> of dashing off to save you from your husband or your
> children or something? I don't know, we've been
> protecting you for years. Did you do that? I don't
> know. I don't know if you really want me to print
> what happened tonight or not....

MAGGIE:

> Henry, how could you say such things to me? You
> have no idea how much you've hurt me. And
> whether you print tonight or not...of course...it's
> up to you....

6. THE FIGHT

PIERRE AND MARGARET ARE DISCOVERED MID-ARGUMENT. ONE MORE TIME THROUGH THE MILL, BUT WITH A DIFFERENCE.

PIERRE:
I received a bill from Creed's the other day. . . .

MAGGIE:
Now we're going to talk about money, but it's not about money, is it, Pierre?

PIERRE:
I also wanted to discuss your relationship with our children. Justin mentioned to me the other day. . . .

MAGGIE:
You were speaking to Justin. . . . You're using the children as spies! I thought I was paranoid, but I'm not paranoid enough for Ottawa.

PIERRE:
I don't understand, we're privileged, you have everything you've always wanted and that continues. I don't understand what could possibly be the matter with you.

MAGGIE:
You're taking away my right to complain! I don't like the beautiful house. I don't like the beautiful job. I don't like what I see happening to you. You're starting to look like those cartoons.

PIERRE:
We explained things to each other. I told you what our life would be like. We made a contract, an agreement. You've just got to be reasonable.

MAGGIE:

Reasonable! Don't say that word, "reasonable." I'm not feeling very "reasonable" tonight. All I can see is that quilt with your motto, "Reason over Passion," written right on it.

She mimes pulling the letters off the quilt and throwing them at him.

Here's an "R" and an "E" and an "A." Look at it! That woman made it for you as a joke. It's all purple and pink. It's got butterflies all over it. It's a joke about a silly man who lives by a silly motto. There's only one motto . . . "Be Here Now."

PIERRE:

Is that what you've come to? Destroying a work of art?

MAGGIE:

After all these years, I don't even know if you're disturbed or not. I want out. I WANT OUT OF CONFEDERATION. I'm sick, sick, sick to death of Canada. You know, John A. Macdonald made a railroad and we made a marriage, and he laid it from East to West, from sea to shining sea . . . . You know, those guys at Confederation, they were drunk. They didn't know what they were doing. John A. put them up to it, and they signed this piece of paper, and we ended up with Canada. I'm sick of timidity and mediocrity, and Bright's Canadian Wine, fake Inuit carving and the Group of Seven! I'm sick of living in a ridiculous country, strung like a clothesline across the American border. Let's admit it; the Americans have always had more fun. Let's go there. No one was meant to live in this climate. Look at you. You're the epitome of a cold land. Let's go someplace warm, where people laugh and cry and

83

hug and shout and dance in the streets. Come on, let's go. I'll pack the kids. We'll just go. Don't call anyone. Say it was all a mistake. Come on, look, we can still make it. I know you want to. Oh, please....
Please....

PIERRE:

You told me you wanted it all. You spoke of shaping destiny. Here is destiny. Feeling like a strong central column, springing from the guts of the land, with two arms outstretched, spanning four thousand miles of diversity and contradiction and space. You and I . . . and the country, involved in a struggle beyond ourselves. This is immortality. Stay with me, stay with me.

MAGGIE:

You almost sucked me in again. You know, through all this, there's only one thing that seems to make any sense at all. Having fun . . . you remember? Having fun?

She dashes off.

7. ENTER MY EMOTIONAL WORLD

HENRY HAS REACHED THE END OF HIS ROPE. HE WANTS PIERRE'S SOUL ON A PLATTER. HE BEGINS BY TRYING TO EXPLAIN THINGS TO THE AUDIENCE.

HENRY:

You have to admit, when she went AWOL, she picked the best. It's become important to me, very important, to find out what he feels. I mean, I watched that guy for nine years. I see him more often than I see my own wife. . . . But that's the story

of my divorce and that's not this one. . . . I mean,
you're always trying to figure out what that tricky
bastard's going to do next. . . and sometimes, you're
even right. Except for this time. I haven't a clue. For
some reason, I have to know if he even cares or not. I
have to. Okay, so let's work it out. . . . So. . .so. . .he's
in his office, right? And you could pick many points
of pain along the way, but let's be cruel. Let's pick
one. Let's pick that weekend. So, he's in his office,
right, and she's just left, and at some point or other,
some poor flack had to make a phone call and say
something like. . . . "Sir, your wife has run off with the
Rolling Stones. You know, 'The Bad Boys of Rock?'
Heroin, court cases. . . . She's staying at the same
hotel, same floor, and she hasn't mentioned you
lately. We just thought you should know." I mean,
what does a man, any man, feel at a time like that?
What did he feel? I have to know. . . .

    PIERRE appears.

PIERRE:
Well, why don't you ask me? Come in. Enter my
emotional world. You may ask me any question
that you choose.

HENRY:
You're on. But I warn you, I'm going to dig
deep. . . . Okay, so that phone call happened. What
was going on inside of you?

PIERRE:
I was alone, she had just left, the phone did ring. . . .

    *He reveals himself for the first time as he listens
on the telephone, shaken, unable to hide the
depth of the impact.*

"No...I...I don't think there's any reason for a statement at this time, thank you." And amid all the pain and fear of being called a cuckold....

He laughs.

...there was an absurd sense of the perfection of the cosmic joke. I mean, a woman with half my intelligence has completely checkmated me. You have to give her credit. It's perfect.

HENRY:
All right. So, it's kind of funny, I got that. But, what else? What does a guy like you do when you're alone and in pain? What did you do that night?

PIERRE:
Do you really want to know?

He closes the curtains and doors.

I wait until I am completely private....

He gets down on his knees.

"In the Name of the Father, and the Son, and the Holy Spirit, Amen. Dear Lord, I am in a state of such complete darkness that I have no idea where to turn, or what the answers are. I humbly beseech your aid in trying to find some way of strength out of this abyss. I also ask you to help me to keep from killing her when she gets back. In the name of the Father, and the Son, and the Holy..."

HENRY:
Oh, no. Not religion. Not a guy like you....

PIERRE:
> You know something, Henry? As we were going
> through all those horrendous fights, my wife was at
> my feet, and she was crying and screaming and
> wailing and literally banging her head against the
> wall, and I stood there, frozen, in the classic pose of
> man, locked in my own gender, not knowing
> whether to go to her and comfort her, or leave
> because it's too personal to watch, or hit her, or what
> to do. And my dominant emotion was jealousy. . .
> that she could be so free. Perhaps that's the tragedy
> of the oppressor. There is a certain joy in it. Perhaps
> for the first time, I feel a part of my entire society . . . .
> The Old World is behind and the New World is a bit
> late in coming, and I ask, with all of us, "What are
> we going to do about marriage?"

> *He breaks the mood.*

> It's worth at least three White Papers. Well, Henry,
> is that what you wanted to see?

HENRY:
> Yeah, yeah.

> *He shakes Trudeau's hand.*

> How do I get out of here?

> *PIERRE indicates the way out. HENRY gets
> his coat, gives a thumbs up signal and leaves.*

8. DISCO—ELECTION

RAUNCHY ROCK MUSIC HERALDS THE NIGHT OF THE MAY, 1979 ELECTION. MARGARET APPEARS IN FULL DISCO REGALIA AND BEGINS TO DANCE THROUGH THE VOICES AND THE ELECTION RESULTS.

Rock music is heard between the voices.

WOMAN'S VOICE:
> Listen, I don't care what she does, but why can't she keep her mouth shut?

MAN'S VOICE:
> I find her totally unattractive. She's a flakey broad, a phony chick.

WOMAN'S VOICE:
> She's put the feminist cause back five years.

MAN'S VOICE:
> Whenever I travel, people ask me about Margaret Trudeau. It's embarrassing. It's a complete drag. She's given Canada a bad name.

ANNOUNCER:
> Liberals, elected two, leading in nine, for a total of eleven. Progressive Conservatives, elected one, leading in four, for a total of five.

WOMAN'S VOICE:
> You know, you can't just do what you want to do. Everybody has to have some responsibilities.

WOMAN'S VOICE:
> What kind of a mother could leave those beautiful children?

ANNOUNCER:
Nationwide standing. Liberals, elected in fifty, leading in fifty-six, for a total of a hundred and six. Progressive Conservatives have now elected fifty-one. They're leading in twenty-four, for a total of seventy-five. No change in Québec, but in Ontario, the Conservatives are making gains. And at least four Cabinet Ministers have gone down to defeat. From the bulk of the returns in from Atlantic and Central Canada, the Conservatives have picked up a net gain of a couple of dozen seats in Southern Ontario, and the Decision Desk is predicting a Progressive Conservative Minority Government.

The music stops.

ANNOUNCER:
Canadian Prime Minister Pierre Trudeau and his Liberal Party have been voted out of office.

MARGARET stops dancing and turns to the audience.

MAGGIE:
All right. So . . . it's Margaret Trudeau, is it? Well, come on. Everybody's up there c their little soap boxes. Who's going to be the first one to stone the whore? That silly bitch . . . . Well, come on . . . . Is it the Mums? The Dads? The kids themselves? The marrieds, the divorced, the Lefties, the Righties? Well, come on, I'm the woman that's offended everybody. Oh, we're so together, aren't we, ladies? We're so on top of it all. We get up in the morning and send the kids off to school, then we get all nice and neat and go off to our really good day job, and we don't mind that all the bosses are still men, noooo . . . . We're handling everything well — in control — we have no problems at all — Ssshhhh . . . .

We come home, pick up the kids from school, and we feed them a delicious dinner of soy beans and spinach — they've never had it so good. And then, hubby comes home and we have intelligent conversation with him — he's never had it so good. And then, at night, we get all foxy and *Vogue* magazine, and we go out and we flirt with the best of them, because we know that's still how you get somewhere. And we're just getting by, just hangin' on . . . just fitting in . . . . Confident smiles . . . . And we're not very silly, are we, ladies? Noooo. And we don't change our minds or blab our faces off. We don't cry or giggle at the wrong moment, do we? Noooo. And we're really good drivers. And, in the midst of all this mastery of the Modern Age, along comes little Maggie Trudeau, doodle-doodle-doo . . . and she falls apart right in the middle of your television set. She says, "I can't cope . . . I don't know if I'm a wife or a mother, or a career . . . or which career. I'm silly and narcissistic . . . I don't . . . I . . . . A husband? . . . I don't know . . . too much . . . I can't cope!   And we don't like that, do we, ladies? Noooo. And we don't like that, do we, gentlemen? Nooooo. Because if Maggie Trudeau, with all the advantages, falls apart, where does that leave us? In the same boat . . . . Welcome aboard. My name is Margaret Trudeau. I'm the woman who gave freedom a bad name. Come on, take a look. I'm not afraid. And I have only one question to ask you . . . . Which do you think is my best feature, my legs . . . or my bum?

MARGARET turns her back and dances away.

The music changes and she becomes HENRY.

9. HENRY'S LAST HURRAH

HENRY'S FIRST LINES ARE INTERCUT WITH A SAD SIXTIES ROCK BALLAD, WHICH FADES AWAY AS HE SPEAKS.

HENRY:

I saw Margaret at McDonald's the other day. I was having an Egg McMuffin and Pepsi. She was sitting there, right as close as you are to me. She didn't recognize me, though, no reason really. She had the kids with her. They were crawling all over her. She never could control them. He came in. He picked up two of the kids, she had the other one, they had an order to go. . . . Then, they both went off in the same car. And I thought. . . well, here I am trying to conclude my assignment. They say I've lost my objectivity. . . and they're right. You see, I have lost something. I've totally lost the ability to judge these people. They come to me and they say, "Marg's stupid," and I go, "Stupid. . . . I haven't even figured out what smart is," and they say, "He's arrogant and corrupt," and they're probably right, but he's given me some really good lines. You see? I've lost it completely. Maybe I've reached the highest level of enlightenment where you can't judge anybody. Except I get this incredible pleasure out of the way those two bug people. It's perverse. Maybe that's the highest level of enlightenment. . . perversity. I don't know. You see, it's like having been involved in one of those incredible thunderstorms, you know the kind? With the flashes and the crashes and the colours. And you stand there, just a bit in awe of all that shit on the line up there. And you don't call it good and you don't call it bad, you're thinking of something else. Then after it reaches one of those heights, it starts to die away. You see a little bit of lightning in the distance, and maybe a crash of thunder, then a little flash of. . . . Maybe a noise over there. . . . Maybe a bit of. . . . No, I see something over. . . . That's me. I'm the guy who can't stop watching.

But you know . . . there's a funny thing about those thunderstorms. . . . You can never quite tell when they're over.

He gives a thumbs up signal to the audience as the lights fade to black.

PRODUCTION NOTES

Because of the way *Maggie & Pierre* was developed in rehearsal, certain production aspects were a more integral part of the play than is usual. Imagine a work process that demanded the "look" of a character in a given scene before it could be written, and you will see the kind of contribution designer Paul Kelman has made. Imagine analyzing a personality through an extensive study of her favourite rock and roll music where we even wrote scenes from the inspiration of that music and you will understand the involvement of Al Higbee.

Also there are something like thirteen costume changes in this one-person extravaganza. They needed to be expertly and quickly executed. Myles Warren working invisibly in awkward backstage circumstances, created a flow essential to the production.

Stage Manager: Myles Warren
Design Assistant and Master Carpenter: Bob Pearson
Assistant to the Lighting Designer: Steve Allen
Audio Research and Production: Al Higbee
Initial Script Preparation: Judy Rudakoff,
Myles Warren and Kit Dawson

Paul Thompson,
Artistic Director,
Theatre Passe Muraille,
Toronto, Ontario.
September, 1980.

Aléola—Gaëtan Charlebois
After Abraham—Ron Chudley
Sainte-Marie Among the Hurons—James W. Nichol
The Lionel Touch—George Hulme
Balconville—David Fennario
Maggie & Pierre—Linda Griffiths
Waiting for the Parade—John Murrell
The Twilight Dinner & Other Plays—Lennox Brown

TALONBOOKS—THEATRE FOR THE YOUNG

Raft Baby—Dennis Foon
The Windigo—Dennis Foon
Heracles—Dennis Foon
A Chain of Words—Irene N. Watts
Apple Butter—James Reaney
Geography Match—James Reaney
Names and Nicknames—James Reaney
Ignoramus—James Reaney
A Teacher's Guide to Theatre for Young People—Jane Howard Baker
A Mirror of Our Dreams—Joyce Doolittle and Zina Barnieh